SLAKKI

Roy Fisher: selected bibliography

POETRY BOOKS BY ROY FISHER

City (Migrant Press, 1961)

Ten Interiors with Various Figures (Tarasque Press, 1966)

The Ship's Orchestra (Fulcrum Press, 1966)

Collected Poems 1968 (Fulcrum Press, 1969)

Matrix (Fulcrum Press, 1971)

The Cut Pages (Fulcrum Press, 1971; Shearsman, 1986)

The Thing About Joe Sullivan: Poems 1971-1977 (Carcanet Press, 1978)

Poems 1955-1980 (Oxford University Press, 1980)

A Furnace (Oxford University Press, 1986)

Poems 1955-1987 (Oxford University Press, 1988)

Birmingham River (Oxford University Press, 1994)

It Follows That (Pig Press, 1994)

The Dow Low Drop: New & Selected Poems (Bloodaxe Books, 1996)

The Long & the Short of It: Poems 1955-2005 (Bloodaxe Books, 2005)

Standard Midland (Bloodaxe Books, 2010)

Selected Poems (Flood Editions, USA, 2011)

The Long & the Short of It: Poems 1955-2010 (Bloodaxe Books, 2012)

Slakki: New & Neglected Poems (Bloodaxe Books, 2016)

ESSAYS / INTERVIEWS / PROSE

Roy Fisher: *Nineteen Poems and an Interview* (Grosseteste, 1975)

Robert Sheppard & Peter Robinson: *News for the Ear:
a homage to Roy Fisher* (Stride Publications, 2000)

John Kerrigan & Peter Robinson (eds.): *The Thing About Roy Fisher:
Critical Studies* (Liverpool University Press, 2000)

Peter Robinson (ed.): *An Unofficial Roy Fisher* (Shearsman, 2010)

Tony Frazer (ed.): *Interviews Through Time* (Shearsman Books, 2013)

Peter Robinson (ed.): *An Easily Bewildered Child: Occasional Prose 1963-2013*
(Shearsman, 2010)

ROY FISHER

SLAKKI

New & Neglected Poems

Edited by
PETER ROBINSON

BLOODAXE BOOKS

ISBN: 978 1 78037 322 5

First published 2016 by
Bloodaxe Books Ltd
Eastburn
South Park
Hexham
Northumberland NE46 1BS

www.bloodaxebooks.com
For further information about Bloodaxe titles
please visit our website or write to
the above address for a catalogue.

Supported using public funding by
ARTS COUNCIL
ENGLAND

Cover design: Neil Astley & Pamela Robertson-Pearce.

Printed in Great Britain by Bell & Bain Limited, Glasgow, Scotland, on
acid-free paper sourced from mills with FSC chain of custody certification.

For Derek and Mary Slade

ACKNOWLEDGEMENTS

Peter Robinson produced and ordered the texts of *Slakki: New & Neglected Poems* responding to the instructions and advice of Roy Fisher. Derek Slade contributed substantially to composing the notes on sources and earlier appearances of the works gathered here. Those notes constitute an extension to the acknowledgements. The first section contains recent poems. The second is a gathering of uncollected poems mainly written during the 1960s, though occasionally foreshadowed later in the previous decade. The third contains poems, similarly uncollected, written in the 1950s.

CONTENTS

THREE

Slakki: Old Norse for a shallow depression among hills. Not much of a valley. A Slack.

ONE

Signs and Signals

When the trench wall came away without warning
and exposed the singularly tall
German officer, set upright in the earth
as if in a raised niche and seeming
unharmed though dead, the sight –
gloves, boots, pale grey-blue greatcoat, attitude –
did its work. For Lance-Corporal (signals) Fisher W., Royal
Fusiliers, it would be the most splendid figure of a man
he'd ever see.

Battered, the cathedral at Reims went some way
towards making up for the soldiery of France
neither stoical nor sanitary.

Then on sunny days
the pleasure of making the sharp flashes of his heliograph
go skittering over the filth for miles.

A Garden Leaving Home

(for Sue Stanford)

One after another the windows that made it gave up looking.
The monitors cut out. No dashes for freedom:
there's always management. The sky
that had cared for the acre since the ocean receded
began taking it back again without comment.

Over a bank where nine
tall old native cherries had oozed, split
and tottered down to pulp the stretch of air
where years of magpies bungled their nests
kept not a memory of all that racket.

The plot filling up fast with curved shapes,
some very small, some moving; brambles
arching above themselves and breaking in waves
down inside the boundary wall. And above,
the patch where design had planted saplings at random
to develop the pretence of a little wood – rowan, field maple, hazel,
goat willow, crab, walnut, sloe – had become
the little wood.

Bureau de Change

For centuries the language has been drawing in its horns:
vowels trimmed back to prevent them from fragmenting,
mutating or singing. Syllables chime and clink quite small. Consonants
polish away often to nothing in the name of adaptability, the human trick:
the world colonised again by way of a thousand airports, no problem, no
      problem.
We walk on pavements rolled from the crushed shells of metaphors.

My task, for an hour, is to deliver
for an audience mostly, like me, without Russian,
helpful translations fashioned for Western ears.
The texts before me are well knit, balanced, clear
as to mood, congenial. The custom these days
is to speak such poetry as if quietly explaining a point in logic.
So, with a nudge here and a pause there,
I can speak these verses in the way I'd speak my own.

That done, the amiable man beside me, appearing
fatigued beyond ever standing upright again,
murmurs his thanks then rises without effort
into an altered state, discernibly magnified
in voice and spirit, head thrown back,
calling out his poems in their own language and
filling the hall with the cry of a cantor, a triumphant pleading.

If those were English words the sounds we're hearing
would need to be a thousand years old.

The Air

in 1960

Out of the air
and back again.
Nowhere to perch. Towers
and half-towers pushed up on the sandstone
balancing fantasy cafés on their corners
with fantasy rooftop vistas across the air.

Experience: by precept and long habit
to avoid if it sits in wait; to evade
if it comes on hard. To absorb
by osmosis without effort. Observed
of an afternoon standing oblique to the crowd
in mild catatonia under a bus-stop canopy
or in the vast hangar of the rag market
sure that among the greasy stalls
was the private oracle that would grab,
not to be evaded, and give a full sight of the engine
that was dropping out grown-up delinquents,
derelicts, junk. And sometimes
in the night places
or on the edge of a party gathered
round an epileptic in a pavement fit
one or two other faces, bewildered
but under compulsion. Writers.

No double depths, no oracle, no
Grand Encounter. Nature
and economics. Just eyes occasionally glinting
from quartz-veins in pebbles, stone scribbles
that didn't need reading. And the year's purpose
breaking apart in gobbets of prose. Accidentals.

Lock Lines for Two Locations

1

working water
held captive for a while
then sluiced away to join
the world's other waters again

2

open
enter and
be lifted safe
with words at your back

3

these doors make depth

power to sink your boat
bodily into the land
and let it go riding out
unharmed

4

step at a time a river
climbs carefully
down through the town

Elsewhere but Overhead

Tea was tea and stuffing stuffing.
They still are. From overhead and nowhere
sake and *blame* arrived. Sake
was slowly-moving flesh: bare skin,
no limbs, no face. It came
to hang in the shadows of the room.
Still does. And blame, likewise unchanged, ready
to slide in as a sloping panel, french-polished,
the colour of stout.

Sky Work

Still suspecting there may be nothing more to itself
than optical tricks and water vapour
it works even harder to be remembered,
colouring its sunsets with particles
from all the barbecues and crematoria of the North.
For me in particular it carves itself alive
into oblongs and squares that stretch
to fit windows exactly; also
freak polyhedrons glimpsed
from doorways and stairwells. Without
feelings of its own it labours to match
whatever moods may float up: the blue
for unbearable bliss; caverns miles deep
in cumulus cities for fortune; limitless grey
for when there's nothing for it but to settle
for a day with indifference for company.
It won't rest.

Bench

(for Peter Robinson)

Varnish and milk
in equal measures. No ideas
but in mixtures, suspensions,
conglomerates, slags
in variety. Apply time, note
when the milk outstinks the varnish.

With my time in my eye
an honorific ode's not on
for one so young, so I'll give you
a piece of my mind: one of the pieces
as it rucks and fissures. In philosophy
ineducable: in observation
passably good, if self-taught.

Sleeping and Thinking and Sleeping

But when it comes down to this cat, he's lying
stretched out on the table across from me
inert, his undefended belly-fur
rising and falling. A paw
thrown loosely over his face to shield
his shut eyes from the light.

That thought's withdrawn. Nobody knows what predators
believe in their long hours away. Just now the merest shrug
has turned his whole head upside down, the skull
pressed flat against the wood,
the exposed eye-slits tight as ever.

He's far from me. From ideas, from alphabets. From
Lights out, and hit the pillow. Now's the time
for a good old think. Gaffes decades old
smoothed over then but still
not rightly analysed. Count and re-check
how many Magrittes I know. Have I
really been getting by on no more than eight?
Is self-plagiarism considered a crime in Belgium?
Strange word, 'chapeau'. Melon I'm allowed
though not from choice; it's grapefruit
that's my forbidden fruit. Could Eve's apple
have been in fact a grapefruit? Cue
an hour-long documentary with a cryptographer,
an iconographer, a theologian, a madman, an
arboriculturist and a pair
of lissom grapefruit-breasted young lady professors. And
by the way, where's my Will?

The cat floats on, out to the wide,
for me to think about all over again.

Smoke and Mirrors

(for Robert Vas Dias)

Smoke and mirrors
make it true

mirrors in gunsmoke-filled
committee-rooms, the glass
yellowed and the silvering holed,
give back to memory
only the true cartoon of those times:
cannonaded walls, smouldering
roof-trusses hanging through the ceilings;
one orderly desk
floating on a pool of bandages;
colours too smeared to read,
a bootstained bandolier,
a cockeyed shako.

1941

Too early in his career for Merleau-Ponty
to have appeared on the syllabus of Wattville Road
Junior Elementary School as I was leaving it
with the bomb-shot windows hanging loose
and the useful part of my education completed

And in any case French Thought
stood not a chance so soon after the Fall.

A matter of waiting a few years once again
for English Blake to uncoil.

Hand-Me-Downs

The nineteenth century of the bizarre
system of dates the Christians have
stands almost empty. Everybody
who helped design the first of the World
Wars is dead, no longer doing much
to anybody; likewise most of the begetters
and settlers-up of the next. They've got
clean away. And so on.

Turnips, four short rows, but enough.
Potatoes, plenty. Kale. For surplus
baby tomatoes, a jar with olive oil
an inch deep over the fruit,
then topped off with aqua vitae,
to rest on the oil and guard it. And
seal tight. And look forward
to winter. Ordinary life,
'restorable' 'normal' 'life' – paraffin,
pepper, fingers that stroke and grip –
sits in the brain like the supreme contemptuous
coinage of disease, nothing more
than a counter devised for murderers to bargain with.

A Mellstock Fiddle

By the road where seldom aught would pass
Save a hearse
He'd, gazing through the blear of the glass,
His comfort seek in verse.

Strange, though, when at the thought of rhyme
Troubles he'd store for himself
As his notebook at an accustomed time
He'd pluck from its trim shelf.

'Twas as though within that withering heart
Some tuneless din
Told what might rule once done was art.
A cat. A biscuit-tin.

A Poetry List

The Appian Way in full swing. Lined
with the marble tombs of the illustrious
dead and rows of crucified gladiators.

Watch Your Step

Then the damned fool decided to write an opera.
He had his reasons; wrote them in the Little Testament. It's still
studied in schools. He learned quickly
that stories of more than an hour
develop a taste for dilemmas, for resolution,
for blood. But he began.

While he was writing his beloved homeland
put itself to the sword once again,
altered its size and shape, reverted
to its former name. His eldest daughter died.

Everybody with a view came to the opera.
It was good. New fame.

From that time on all the austere
earlier works – the keyboard Scintillae,
the unforgiving String Quartets, even
the Cassation for mismatched Hardanger fiddles –
had to submit to change: irrecoverably and forever
stained through with opera juice.

A Number of Escapes and Ways Through

The first came
with the conviction of a divided dusk, one path
deflected sideways and up to an evening
charged with lost lights,
everything in it that might float out or be fished for
of even clout. Equal, unranked, free for the taking.

Then arranging to forget
the known lie of the land beyond the next bend
and watching the void fill rapidly with enough inventions
to bring reality to its knees.

I created everything I see.
It wasn't hard. And with
crusts of detail I could never have guessed at.
Soon gone: even
the name of the relevant *philosophe*
got rinsed away with the rest of it.

It seems
nobody thought of trying to steal Roger Langley
or borrow him for a spell.
Already and always at home elsewhere.

Todor Zhivkov
a man in a jar
trapped for four seconds in a TV screen
decades ago and never escaping,
mouthing silent lies, his face
the precipitate and stain of the violent collision
of opposed understandings. His bad luck to be caught so:
could have been anybody.

While There's Still Time

While there's still time to make dispositions
I want it put about that when I come back
it won't be, as you might have been supposing,
as a cat or a capybara. No: I shall return
in the form of a nut-brown silver-banded
bassoon. If I'm in the care
of a woman with good lungs and long smooth arms
so much the better. I'm certain she'll let nothing
stand in the way of her playing me
for a series of solo recitals on the tarmac triangle
at the crook of Kentish Road where the lorries
used to wait for the great gates of the Carriage Works
to open and let them through. Make no mistake:
my voice will be heard once again,
and as never before.

TWO

The Estuary

There is no shore!
where should be sand
and mile-long
tumbled strips of river littoral,
where should be water-birds
and the firm, vertical
breakwater and bank,
the shallow tide has spread
shivering on a sunlit afternoon
to the very lip of the land
and holds there still,
straining above itself
when the rich light-beams slip
through brief tarnishes of cloud
so that houses across the water
lie hull-down dancing white on the back of the hand
impersonal, sinister,
a mere idea.

Heroic Landscape

A muttering grey sky
        shallow hopeless canopy
Rolled down right to its whitened
Rim around the horizon
                where the low
Black hills of nightmare start that stretch
To the world's own lip maybe

Here round-limbed long-haired
        women inhabit only
With horses and slow cattle
The staring green-gold pastures
                 among ponds
That glimmer under the winds as they
Feel their way in from the west

And the boy just born
        sprawling ruddy and fatherless
On the menacing grass where he falls
Laughs out loud as the sky though slime
                  still hears him
And out of him the cord still glistens
Tangled cerulean-silver

Divisions

On these exhausted slopes
The snow has lain three days now in clear light,
Mottled on roofs, dragged to roll thick in launders,
In gardens clotted, on clay fields
Spread like a pelt.

Out of the valley floor
Close by a ramp where hoppers lurch
The red-lead girders of a half-built factory
Jut under sketched white lines
Ominous and bare.

And on the hill behind
The snow-scarves tear on red clay knuckles,
On dull walls strung like wagons,
And tile-red peaks
Despondent in the dry white element.

Complaint

I can recall no longer
the face I've pictured once too often.

I would like some critic, however bad,
to say once more what poetry is:

like shrivelled changelings
the verses of my friends and masters
squint at me from their pages.

Three Moments

The flange on the edge of the board
exists for you by now
more than it does for me:

having run it our swiftly
from the mere sound, flange,
I've had no time to look at it, as yet;

it must be like the legs
that are so surely moving
those high hard steps out there in the darkness.

Night Walkers

Darkness hisses at the town-blocks' end.
Salt-glaze of sleet
Pocks fingers, coldly grits the walks
Sprung flat, like table-knives.

There's a smashed box of wind in every street,
And lamps, for startled hours,
Wistfully guard
Behind their glistening panes shaken with blows
The blanched gold cheeks
Of those we seek for miles sardonically.

Script City

Now let me drag the night
Across us like a table,
Over the stove and the fire-irons,

Over the acid light it smothers,
The black shrubs in the forecourt
And our cloudy quiet.

Sleep with me in the ghost
The lamp shed on the dark,
And I'll see that we wake

Late, in a marine city
Strung newly across the bay,
Its white blocks wet with fog;

A place where, quietly,
All scripts are made, and figures,
And words lie down to sleep as we do.

Something Unmade

There's something unmade
in the street this morning.

The wind at the door
comes straight from licking at it,

and the thicket of noise
contains a new silence.

Something more delicate
than an egg on the tarmac,

more quiet and bland
than the milk in the bottle,

prouder than housetops.

If I walk out now
before the street's busy,

kicking a newspaper
rolled in a ball

with under one arm
a musical instrument,

it may find things easier.

I would not have it
left there to grow fractious.

Results

Sitting in cafés
For years on end
I have given a certain justice of the eye
To a few things:

To four or five of the glances
Cast my way,
To the loves and indecisions and so forth
Of friends and not-friends.

Now they come around
Like fish in a stream;
Linger a moment for recognition
And leave, unharmed.

Last Brief Maxims

Judge by colours.
Consult the breast,
The groin, the belly;
Make things you can carry.

At each day's end
Laugh at the clock
And die in the squat
Wall of the honeycomb.

Study anatomy.
Sacrifice often
To the weather and women;
Make room for the dead.

Consider how
A second glance
Denies the first
Denies the first.

After Midnight

The lamps that clamber
About the moon,
The pinnacles and the parapets.

August carries
A cold in its belly,
After the crowds
Bloated clowns lie in the leaves.

The lamps that clamber
About the moon,
The pinnacles and the parapets.

Traffic lights
Wind down the hours;
An early fog
Filters across the public face.

The lamps that clamber
About the moon,
The pinnacles and the parapets.

An open eye.
Eroded streets.
Trying the doors
A constable finds night unlocked.

Motion

Arching but not quite met.
Inconsistent. Rub
harder. It can't: you can't – 'I
Can, am, and have.'

Terrible leaves
Drop flowers like
Terrible berries
Under themselves.

What urgency? Beat
Blunted across the bows
By water bar.
Two tongues in one mouth,
Limited struggle and
love-legs.

It passes.
Cables pass over the fields,
The papery fields:
Treads of grime get
printed out.

The Discovery of Metre

Moving towards
  the multiplication
    of fields
The respectful
  population of his
    surroundings by himself
His tokens
  understood
    his work done
By others without bidding
  his newest thoughts
    read in advance
He took to talking
  at length
    and like
Any old man
  walking downstairs
    three steps
And a pause
  still talking
    pleased to be
Talking and
  still making it
    downstairs.

Abraham Darby's Bridge

Forget the masterpiece itself:
it cracks with watching;
a slow landslide
shoves at the pier-stones

and the black spars
of the ironwork built like joinery,
cranking the arch out
with a wader-bird's leverage

meet to support less – only
a tarred, spongy walk
without even the trade
of a tourist's fee.

The masterpiece is now
a standing elegy
masking its old truculence:
anyway, *that* past is shot.

Yet how we love a bridge –
bay-breaker or ditchplank,
a dry-eyed span –
Forget the thing itself, though,

now that it has to be
torn down for safety
or turned to a monument;
reverie all that can conjure

the bustle of the gorge then,
cargoes on the Severn,
smoke among the bluffs, sooty chimneys
starting from the wood:

now an empty railbed
tracks up the river's course
past Coalport and Madeley –
rubbles of the enterprise

with gardens and hovels
collapsed into peace,
patched with fresh mortar,
with fresh cinders.

The sky opens to the north,
rods bow under elders;
on the valley, scorch-marks
look small and honourable.

But spit into the wind,
the century after next returns it:
to the played-out heap
colonies are coming.

Variations

(on Bag's Groove*)*

Somewhere
under cool
parallels
        breath

a strike
between fingers
and silver sound
        globes

touch
sourness thrusting
expansion
        hollow
        and clean

Plangent
descends on
lead steps
        talking

dirt
shifts with ease
on a simple
        river

flavour
from a movement
darkly metallic
        open.

Inside this
    shining vastness
    men
walk, their steps rustling
around quick stabs of talk;
    they move on concrete
    and iron treads;
their sleep narrows away
in the distance of sound

The city's eye
closes on some
still moving
through deserted quarters
trading blankness
with the streetlamps' rings

Stays shut before
grey wind on paving stones
stairways in progress
and demolitions

If we shake the unending town
this way and that across
its entwining avenues
    can we keep
the coins that fall?

Scents
    shiver
        pains
down this
mineral world
frozen
where as by accident
we find blood running

And there's a line of garden
patches with tulip leaves

                    there are
enough cells open
        boxes
                    kiosks enough
cells

This needle finds you and
this
        needle
drinks.

Hollow
and loosened
music around
        this movement

closing
unbroken on
torn and distorted
        faces

man
curving the lidless
night between
        cool parallels.

The Bachelors Stripped Bare by Their Bride

A.B.C. 'The three of us discussed your masterpiece – '

D.   'Splendid, my boys! I don't know whether – '

A.B.C. 'And we decided we should like to ask – '

D.   'It overheard you; it and I are no longer on
the best of terms. I have – '

A.B.C. 'How far you feel your concept still holds good.'

D.   'an idea it disapproves of the use I made of what
it earned me. That was a happy time!'

A.   'Would you, for instance, do the same again?'

D.   'I couldn't, if I tried. I'm senile. I'm happy too;
besides, this is a most progressive age and I spend
all my time with these little ...'

B.   'Your work was hailed in nineteen-ten as being – '

D.   'They said all sorts of things. I remember
there were two red-haired brothers – '

C.   'And some of us have still not quite caught up!'

D.   'My dear young friends, remember this: I am a very
elderly Frenchman. The thing
that has interested me most through my life
is eroticism. God bless us all.'

A.B.C. 'That doesn't quite – '

D.   ' – Including you. Goodnight.'

THREE

Double Morning

This long inconstant waking to a day
Hung round with clouds, fouled with dark smears of rain
   On passive walls of grey
That spent-out gusts obscurely trouble,
Makes a contented window, whose wide pane
Looks two ways on a world made double;
Uncertain day, uncertain dream.

I wake under wings, among such wraps
As yield to dawn's murk imperceptibly;
   My limbs succeed to histories that lapse
Slow-fingered into the giant holes of night,
From their persuasions loosing me,
Comforted in this ashen world to remember them:
Dreams of an unknown freedom and appetite.

For I have been through and still am moist from it
Some place of birth in that last untroubled plain of sleep:
   A misted, populous marl-pit
   Where the body's made whole;
And countless human limbs lie folded deep,
Growing in ease under a silvered rain,
In dream-earth's strange and common bowl
Denuded of identity and pain.

Division of Labour

I saw the dustmen drink the light
And remain dry;
I saw the grey wagon of desiccation,
While the day raced in rivulets all about it,
Crawling along the gutter like a blind dog.

I thought of an endless night, so deep
That it would slake them,
These parched and red-eyed men,
In flooded shafts and cool sky-valleys:
I wanted them to love that blue mind
For all of us, whose claim on it was less.

Then saw how they were decomposed
Into their dust,
The skin losing its touch and the eyes their distance,
So that they hardly sensed
Even the ripples under the girders of the bridge
They crossed at nightfall going home;

And I remembered how our dreams
Can make themselves only
From what we touch when we are wide awake.

I saw the dustmen drinking light
And the grey wagon of desiccation
crawl in the gutter like a blind dog.

The Lover

Iron soaked by rain
Was what I found,
   The idea of purity I wanted
To cleanse the gross involvements
Of my thick fancy
   Where everything I loved
Was spoiled, made heavy
   With my possessing it.

    To think of this wet metal
   Was to shed passivity;
If I imagined the taste of it
   I was strong.

That clarity I looked for, though
Either has no body or must be
   Some lighter element:
This thing's not always welcome,
   My choice was flawed,
And now, everywhere in my mind,
   That sullen weight, that naked flavour,
Hector and madden me.

Silence

Each of my solitudes
Should be, as some of them are,
A cylinder of decision.

When the face stays
Mouthless
The birds are seen moving.

So great was my quiet
I have laughed at the faces
I made up among the trees.

And sometimes it would last
Even beyond my strength,
Breeding new pleasure;

Frictions would break in
Agreeably, like
The gradual inroads of sleep about my body.

*

More often I would fold up my head
Like a soiled tablecloth,
Put it away

And dwindling downwards,
Stump about
Innocently heavy.

*

Giant legs of stone
Can become old men's
Crumpled trousers.

'Neighbours, We'll Not Part Tonight!'

(The Demon Knitters of Dent)

Roll me round to the stories of the great knittings
that took place in the foretimes
in a smell of straw and peat in smoky kitchens

with a 'clack' for a sound
we're knitting the houses round

As the sun's great sheep's eye slunk down behind the fell
and his thick grey blanket folded its long rows over
door after door closed soft as the mighty strode,
staggered, ran, limped in the dark to their knitting spell

with a step for a sound
we're knitting the houses round

There was Ramsback Rachel, Black Tick and Tam Tup,
Six-Pin Tirleyman (twisty Gannelbon's grandson)
Little Stitch Baby and Kitty Curl, Granny Pullock with the straddle legs
and a long pale idiot man who would knit with his toes: these made the
          party up

with a breath for a sound
we're knitting the houses round

Then came the girls Pocket and Flitty, and Ribber Wagstaff with his
          strong thumbs,
Giantess Appleyard in ten petticoats and not perspiring
and Schoolmaster Weazell with his knitted walking-stick
come to set all the children their knitting sums

with a squeeze for a sound
we're knitting the houses round

Where was the clicking of laughter than but amid the smoke
when the knitting songs and the knitting stories ran free
and the mutton-grease fumbled the wool
and the wool-swaddled babes in the cockloft started to choke?

With a cough for a sound
we're knitting the houses round

When it's long past midnight and the yards of knitting enfold
foot upon stamping foot, not gingerly pressed together
and the flushed pink faces still mouth out the rows of song
then the joy of the knitting runs stitches through young and old

with a gasp for a sound
we're knitting the houses round

Then the needles fly faster and faster: wondrous rows fall
like foam on the beck from those long-labouring fingers;
pile on the floor to the last knitting hymn round knees, waists, bosoms
            and clasp
all the great passionate ones in one soft breathing pall

with a sociable silence
we're knitting the houses round

Unravelling

My mind is full of images of comfort:
would you like a few?
A cushion, a lane, a granny with a perambulator?

> They bring me up short
> like the stares of cows across gates.

The whole world is equally padded. Now
how about a gas-mask?

> That's baleful.

An arrowhead?

> Flushed with sunrays.

A desire?

> That's like a fish, and twists and turns
> in a void it's somehow made. Again:

Do you need it again?

> I need
> a pinewood wall on a rainy evening.

Anything else you might like?

> Now
> you're talking.

A Gift of Cream

Among the angles of dead light
The nuns consume a winter gift of cream.

At thigh-level, the weight of the company
Lies out in seated, shifting horizontals
In a variety of flesh colours suggesting
Sun and cheeses: shifting horizontals, so quiet,
The plank thighs of marionettes
Hidden in fretting, voluminous skirts,
Thornless, unsuffering, sisters among
With a dark tone of shine on china,
Thighs hidden, rejoicing a little,
Swimming sideways and together
In the sister whiteness.

A battery, and quietly
Hushed a distant barrage of coughs
Barracks the sweetness enjoyed
And remembered, with cheese still in the mouth,
Sunlight on fur, a garden chair painted blue, and others.

A room of women's thighs was not foreseen.

La Magdalena

Magdalen, white witch,
Dancing by starlight
Became before dawn
The guitar on my table.

No woman sign or accent
Was there that morning:
A half-made spell
Fallen to music.

Two years, or two hundred
The song was perfecting:
Still chords held fading love,
Stars shone in daylight;

Till by the touch of strings,
Each moving tremor,
I knew my five songs
Truer than reasons.

Then, in distress of heart,
Gladness of music,
I loosed this Magdalen,
Her spell completing.

The Doctor Died

A bad fly bit him. There in the soft hillocks through the olive
arch behind his breast, that gold-and-green angular fly from
the laughing parrot-woods laid its own chuckle with a jab and
a pinch, an acidulous finger for a moment probing his banks;
then the coloured poison mounted him, the contented cloud
shapes like pink cake, the concealed blood seeping as through
wonderful sponge, the leathery towers and bastions of his creamy
old youth began to crumble down into white sheets, shooting
in folds down his gristly bending skeleton. The cochineal blood
runnelled down to his boot-feet, the amber water running
afterwards; he stood on dark weights, and the blue phalanges
of his fingers did a flick, like fat caterpillars. The falling-down
of his back pulled up his head, a rose-coloured, ready-to-cry
head in the sunshine. Under the polish of his chin, in mauve
caves, blond bristles jerked outwards and outwards, and the
bones of his mouth braced themselves and shone. Then what
shouts curved out across the mustard-green hillocks, swinging
the windmills round and round in the blue over the hilltops!
The dusty groundsel grew quicker about his sliding ham-feet,
and the clump-trees whistled their gulls home early. The poison
danced and beat in the thick shoulders and he groaned in tenor
despair; his gold glasses fell off and his blue eyes looked down
on his face that shuddered like a cliff. He saw the muscle
revolving round his white mouth, and the slow action of his
nostrils; he saw the blond hairs start from his cheeks and shrivel
into a salad of bleached worms as they reached the air; he saw
the oval islands of fat running across beneath the slackened
skin of his chest; through the roof of his merely filmed ribs, he
saw, far below, the vitreous ocean-basin of his belly, shimmering
in furnace colours, and the glowing bread bones of his legs like
trees in dark tunnels of fire. Beneath him in the ground were
beds of gold and emeralds hammering up at him, many eyes
winking and blasting back at his stare.

The sun thrust its muzzle from behind into the rearing mass and shoved it forward a yard onto a red parsley-bush. It melted down through the curved twigs, the skin pricked up across the top, tautening in the afternoon sun like a yellow bag, sagging still as it drained, and with its still-solid pink head staring down among the crimson roots.

Piano

(to Luis Buñuel)

Abandoned by Apollo's tide,
his rock-pool, moonlight,
there sprawls far out on a crag
a man in evening dress,
the sharp and careful pines
feathering his loneliness.

Aloft, beyond this faint musician,
safe in stony shelter,
his turbulent machine
sleeps, by giants' tumbled bones
and mountain cold guarded,
a slumberous shining carapace
that gapes by daylight to reveal
light clangours on slim strings
of steel and copper; harmonies
exhaling the sudden stench
and spirit of a strident animal –
Onager in the desert, running
riotous amid the scrub,
an ass who kicked and killed,
yet now is tamed to holy functions –
over a ring of hooves
his teeth flash in the music mouth,
those red and jewelled eyes glitter
at each clatter of keys.
As laden slaves sweat upwards
lash hums like a fly about
God in his ebony ark
while human muscles strain the beast,
the engine to its singing mountain:

Klondike-Popocatepetl,
volcano of gold,
sees him established, heavenly,
by a nameless *padrona*.
 – Or sea-brine saps his banded legs,
though to his candy tunes
sad parasols revolve
and every foam-fraught girl
whispers her name to his flagging master:

Onager's island soul lies
caged in copper wires now, greenly.

Far from the wall of pines and the steaming hill
always the turns of the algae and the walking
sands of the sea escape our square white fingers.

The Moral

Home from the funeral, the horses and gilded cars,
Prince Androgyne, searching for almonds, found
A frog and a ferret asleep in a jasper vase.

It was surely a portent: already now mourning-dim,
His ecstatic eyes blossomed in tears, which, falling like stars,
Caused the oblivious pair to be deftly drowned,
Engulfing the pointed head and each furry limb
And all of the frog, who knew perfectly well how to swim.

A Conceit for the Empress

Points and spangles of light lacing darkness
In the cavernous room there as sidling courtiers wink
Never and retreat in search of themselves,
And the great lamp of her stands, ornate,
Golden, or brazen, or gilt; no movement needed,
Her many decorations hang, fine, or tawdry, or gilt,
Having neither taste nor shame, her flame informing each.

A Vision of Four Musicians

The village will soon forget them, and how they came wandering
As if by chance through the crowd, in clothes the colour of earth;
Stopping unasked, and playing tenuous music
That rose in the heat-haze, suspended, hovering
Fragile as an echo from the journey they came or the path
They had yet to travel; ancient measures, wavering,
Drawn by lean hands from the weathered strings and wood.

Now they are gone; yet the strangely anonymous faces
Remain in the mind: the dancing villagers' coins and bread
They refused, quietly, surely disappearing,
Already less substantial than when they arrived;
Their coming called into doubt the harvest horizon
As if soon they would vanish completely, leaving the faded voices
High in the air behind them, striving still to be heard.

To see them in fields where the blissful vision
Is undisturbed; pursue that field where the mild heraldic
Creatures sport, free of their myths: the ghostly musician,
Gryphon, and the unicorn, lost his Avenger and Maiden, dissolved
In a friendly sky; to abandon these formulae, learn the hieratic
Art: – but here are avenger and maiden, dancing, prepared;
Become them, but offer no victim: never hear music.

Roy Fisher on the Nature of Neglect

I describe the poems in sections two and three as neglected. I must emphasise that these poems have not been passed over or slighted by publishers, editors or reviewers: indeed my work always seems to me to have had as much attention as it deserved or was likely to get. The neglect has been entirely mine.

The juvenilia of poets often exhibit an excess of urgency combined with a lack of direction. My own period of juvenilia was of this character. It started late, at about twenty, and lasted for over a decade, disabled throughout by a technical shortcoming which I was to recognise only in retrospect long after it had quietly solved itself. It was that my poems lacked a stable self: the character who was writing the poem and responsible for it and to it. My everyday self – a quite presentable, penurious and apparently unambitious young man – created no problems, but the self that should have been present or implicit in what I wrote was something of a weak ankle. Required to bear weight it would shift stance and not be answerable. A series of vestigial stock figures stood in, no more than grammatical fictions. And throughout the period there was an area of my mind that was occupied by a slowly-evolving costume drama guided by meticulously recorded dreams and dominated by myths, psychoanalysis, serial metaphors, fantasies, often morbid, hallucinations, fixations and guesswork. All this material propelled me towards writing; and although I was in sympathy with modernism and its derivatives it didn't occur to me to align my work with those movements. Anything that looked like a poem would do, however strident or archaic.

Occasionally, though, I would give myself the slip and write more casual pieces, invariably begun from chance operations. These were taken up immediately. I couldn't understand why as they seemed to me very flimsy, but they have remained at the centre of later collections. Some examples of this kind which I had to leave because I lacked skills to do them justice are here included, but I think they show the beginning of a thread that has persisted through almost everything I've done since.

The theme of neglect came alive with the prospect of issuing a collection. Coming late to the idea of seeing my work between covers, I had, and have, little feel for the business of publishing books; and it was only the shrewd eye of Stuart Montgomery of Fulcrum Press that saw how a pared-down version of my gathered magazine appearances could make a coherent book. My contribution was to add a level of self-censorship. With no new work at all in prospect it seemed likely this volume would be my only book of poems, at once an introduction and a valediction, and I worked, with an eye to the vicious reviewing climate of the time, to simplify its profile, cutting out cross-currents, duplications and poems that needed a stronger supporting context. By this time I had for years been able to be confident in what I'd been doing, while understanding that the work, of its nature, would look outlandish or gauche, and I wanted its character to show out. The result of our editing was a carefully constructed slim volume which Stuart with some irony issued as *Collected Poems 1968*. The cut material was left to lie unexamined again until now. That turn of events furnishes the majority of the neglected items in the present volume.

There's an element of what could better be called habitual negligence that also has a bearing. Ten years on the outlook in my corner of the poetry world was less propitious. I was writing again and being usefully anthologised and interviewed. But adventurous publishers from the Sixties had gone out of business with a new generation hardly begun; a particular loss was the publisher of my first four books. A couple of long-running feuds and vendettas, destructive of friendships and collaborations, were available for those who found them nourishing. I had no publisher. When people wanted to read me I was reduced to sending out photocopies of out-of-print publications; I was not keeping records or making copies; I was giving readings from manuscript sheets in large handwriting. It will have been at this time that Derek Slade, not yet known to me, must have surmised that I was not a fit person to be left in charge of my own writings and began, unasked, to track and list them, beginning his invaluable Bibliography.

Tired of this state of affairs, mistrustful of the uncertain fortunes of small presses and in need of a Collected Poems, I eventually accepted an approach from an august general publisher which had no reputation for dynamic marketing and was likely to keep my works, bundled together between covers, available in the warehouse for a considerable time. My expectations were not high and my faith in books as works of art had been weakened; but the resulting volume was a disgraceful botch with editorial good intentions parsimoniously overridden at a late stage, cheap paper and crowded page layouts. I had my bundle: but in order to get it into print I had sold my poems down the river. And there they were to remain for the next fifteen years, till I could return them to the care of specialist publishers.

NOTES

ONE

13: 'Signs and Signals': (2013) first published in *1914: Poetry Remembers*, ed. Carol Ann Duffy (London: Faber & Faber, 2013).

14: 'A Garden Leaving Home': (December 2014) first published in *Hwaet!: 20 Years of Ledbury Poetry Festival*, ed. Mark Fisher (Hexham: Bloodaxe Books & Ledbury Poetry Festival, 2016).

15: 'Bureau de Change': (2012) previously unpublished in English. First appearance, translated into Russian, in *Iz nesabyvshish menya* [From those who remember me], an anthology of poems in honour of Joseph Brodsky, ed. Valentina Polukhina and Andrey Olear (Tomsk, 2015).

16: 'The Air': (2012) first published in *Jubilee Lines: 60 Poets for 60 Years*, ed. Carol Ann Duffy (London: Faber & Faber, 2013).

17: 'Lock Lines': (2012) first published in *Locklines* (Canal & River Trust and Chrysalis Arts; no date of publication given, but *c.* 2012/2013).

18: 'Elsewhere but Overhead': (2010) previously unpublished.

19: 'Sky Work': (September 2015) previously unpublished.

20: 'Bench': (2012) first published in *Peter Robinson at 60*, ed. Adam Piette, *Blackbox Manifold* 9 (2012).

21: 'Sleeping and Thinking and Sleeping': (December 2013) previously unpublished.

22: 'Smoke and Mirrors': (2010) first published in *Entailing Happiness: Friends of Robert Vas Dias*, ed. Maggie Butcher (London: Infinity Press; distributed by Permanent Press, 2010).

23: '1941': (April 2015) previously unpublished.

24: 'Hand-Me-Downs': (1993) first published in *Klaonica: Poems for Bosnia* (Bloodaxe Books and *The Independent*, 1993), in *The Dow Low Drop: New & Selected Poems* (Bloodaxe Books, 1996), and *The Arts of Peace: An Anthology of Poetry*, ed. Adrian Blamires and Peter Robinson (Two Rivers Press and the English Association, 2014).

25: 'A Mellstock Fiddle': (2006) first published in *Answering Back*, ed. Carol Ann Duffy (London: Picador, 2007).

26: 'A Poetry List': (January 2008) first published in *An Unofficial Roy Fisher*, ed. Peter Robinson (Exeter: Shearsman Books, 2010).

27: 'Watch Your Step': (2014) previously unpublished.

28: 'A Number of Escapes and Ways Through': (January-February 2016) previously unpublished.

29: 'While There's Still Time': (2014) previously unpublished.

TWO

33: 'The Estuary': (1958) first published in *Samphire*, 12 May 1971.

34: 'Heroic Landscape': (1958) first published in *An Unofficial Roy Fisher*, ed. Peter Robinson (Exeter: Shearsman Books, 2010).

35: 'Divisions': (1960) first published in *An Unofficial Roy Fisher*, ed. Peter Robinson (Exeter: Shearsman Books, 2010).

36: 'Complaint': (1960) first published in *Mica* 2 (February 1961).

37: 'Three Moments': (1957) first published in *Samphire*, 12 May 1971.

38: 'Night Walkers': (1960) first published in *Living Arts*, 1, 1963, as part of *City*, though this poem was not included either in the Migrant Press edition (1961) or the subsequent revised edition.

39: 'Script City': (1960) first published in *Poetry and Audience*, 9:7 (1961-62).

40: 'Something Unmade': (1960) first published in *Poetry and Audience*, 9:7 (1961-62).

41: 'Results': (1960) first published in *An Unofficial Roy Fisher*, ed. Peter Robinson (Exeter: Shearsman Books, 2010).

42: 'Last Brief Maxims': (1960) first published in *An Unofficial Roy Fisher*, ed. Peter Robinson (Exeter: Shearsman Books, 2010).

43: 'After Midnight': (1960) first published in *Sixty-One* (February 1962).

44: 'Motion': (1968) first published in *Grosseteste Review* 1:2 (Autumn 1968)

45: 'The Discovery of Metre': (1964) first published in *An Unofficial Roy Fisher*, ed. Peter Robinson (Exeter: Shearsman Books, 2010).

46: 'Abraham Darby's Bridge': (1966-70) first published in *New Poems 1971-72: A PEN Anthology of Contemporary Poetry*, ed. Peter Porter (London: Hutchinson, 1972).

48: 'Variations (on *Bag's Groove*)': (1957) first published in *Beat Dreams and Plymouth Sounds: an Anthology*, ed. Alexis Lykiard (Devon: Plymouth Arts Centre, 1987).

51: 'The Bachelors Stripped Bare by their Bride': (1960) first published in *Curtains* 1 (1971).

THREE

55: 'Double Morning': (1955), first published in *Delta* 10 (August 1956).

56: 'Division of Labour': (1961) first published in *An Unofficial Roy Fisher*, ed. Peter Robinson (Exeter: Shearsman Books, 2010).

57: 'The Lover': (1957) first published in *Migrant* 5 (March 1960).

58: 'Silence': (1957) first published in *Combustion* 4 (1957).

59: '"Neighbours, We'll Not Part Tonight!"': (1957) first published as part of a collaboration with artist Astrid Furnival for Ronald King's Circle Press (Guildford, 1976).

61: 'Unravelling': (1957) first published in *Curtains* 1 (1971).

62: 'A Gift of Cream': (1955) first published in *Origin* 20 (1955).

63: 'La Magdalena': (1953) broadcast on radio programme *Signature*, Western Region Service, 13 July 1955. First print publication is the present volume.

64: 'The Doctor Died': (1954) first published in *Three Early Pieces* by Roy Fisher (London: Transgravity Press, 1971).

66: 'Piano': (1953) first published in *Three Early Pieces* by Roy Fisher (London: Transgravity Press, 1971).

67: 'The Moral': (1952) first published under the title 'Hough! Hough!' in *Mermaid* 19:1 (January 1953).

68: 'A Conceit for the Empress': (1951) first published in *Mermaid* 19:1 (January 1953).

70: 'A Vision of Four Musicians': (1951) first published in *Mermaid* 18:1 (October 1951).